FOR THE LOVE OF
Research

By Murray Suid
Illustrated by Corbin Hillam

This book is for Del Alberti.

Publisher: Roberta Suid
Editor: Elizabeth Russell
Cover Design: David Hale
Design and Production: Susan Pinkerton
Cover Art: Corbin Hillam

monday morning®

Monday Morning is a registered trademark
of Monday Morning Books, Inc.

Entire contents copyright © 1986 by Monday Morning
Books, Inc., Box 1680, Palo Alto, California 94302

ISBN 0-912107-50-2

Printed in the United States of America

9 8 7 6 5 4

Contents

Introduction   4

Part I. Skills

Research Fundamentals   5
   The Fact Finder Play   6

Asking Questions   11
   Can You See a Question?   12
   Question Collecting   13
   Two Kinds of Questions   14

Exploring the Library   15
   What's in the Library?   16
   Dewey Decimal Speeches   17
   Dewey Decimal Book Hunt   20
   Dewey Decimal Posters   21
   Reading a Catalog Card   22
   Reference Book Speeches   23
   Bulletin Board   24

Using Books   25
   Reading a Contents Page   26
   Reading an Index   27
   Reading a Bibliography   28
   Reading a Fact Table   29
   Taking Notes   30

Learning from People   31
   Finding Experts   32
   Model Interview   33
   Interview Planner   34
   Pet Poll   35
   Research Letter   36

Observing   37
   Knowing What to Look For   38
   Alike and Different   39
   Drawing What You See   40
   High and Low Temperature Graph 41
   Attendance Graph   42

Giving Reports   43
   Report Checklist   44
   Model Report   45
   Bulletin Board Checklist   46

Part II. Projects

Library Scavenger Hunts   47
   Reference Book Hunt   48
   Quotation Hunt   49
   What Does It Look Like?   50
   Mystery Maps   51
   Finding All Kinds of Facts   52

Double-checking the Facts   53
   What's the Real Story?   54

Trivia   55

No-copying Encyclopedia Reports   56

Destination: Earth!   58
   A Visit to the Planet Earth   59
   Poll About Space Visitors   60
   Earth Places   61
   Earth People   62

Classroom Reference Shelf   63

Answer Key   64

Introduction

A fact in itself is nothing. It is valuable
only for the idea attached to it, or for the
proof which it furnishes.
    Claude Bernard

Rather than love, than money, than fame,
give me truth.
    Henry David Thoreau

Recall the old parable: Give people fish and you feed them for a day; teach them to fish and you help them overcome their hunger forever.

It's the same story with learning. Teach students facts and they'll remember just those facts...maybe. Teach them to *find* facts, and there are no limits to what they'll discover.

This book aims to help you teach students to become fact finders.

Part I—Skills—introduces the fundamentals of research in a short play called "The Fact Finder." Following the play are lessons dealing with six key tasks: asking questions, using the library, learning from books, interviewing experts, observing, and giving reports. Each lesson centers around one or more *reproducible worksheets*.

Part II—Projects—provides challenging and entertaining ways for students to use their growing research skills. Activities range from information scavenger hunts to studying Earth from an extraterrestrial point of view.

An annotated bibliography suggests several invaluable books for a classroom reference shelf.

Good luck with building your students' love of research, but remember what Horace said nearly two thousand years ago:

To know all things is not permitted.

Research Fundamentals

GOAL:
Helping students understand research

ACTIVITIES:
1. To introduce the research process, have students read aloud or perform *The Fact Finder*. This duplicatable five-page script teaches that research starts with questions. It also dramatizes the three ways to answer research questions: using books and other "fact packages," interviewing people, and observing for oneself. For reinforcement, have your students perform the play for younger students.
2. To show that all sorts of people—not just students—use research, invite a variety of researchers as classroom guests. Try lawyers, newspaper reporters, business owners, writers, realtors, doctors, and teachers.

The action takes place near the library.

Characters

Book	Magazine	Sports writer
Customer	Newspaper	Student
Fact Finder	Reporter	Trainer

Student: Yuck! Groan! Boo-hoo! I hate doing research!

(After some sort of fanfare or drum roll, a character appears wearing a T-shirt with the words "Fact Finder" printed on it.)

Student: Who are you?

Fact Finder: Can't you read?

Student: Oh, are you Fact Finder?

Fact Finder: That's a good guess. My job is to show people how to love research, not hate it. Now what was all that groaning and boo-hooing about?

Student: I have to give a boring report in school.

Fact Finder: What's your subject?

Student: Ice cream.

Fact Finder: Ice cream sounds interesting.

Student: Interesting to eat, maybe, but boring to learn about. It means going to the library and copying a bunch of stuff from a bunch of books.

Fact Finder: Who says you've got to do that?

Student: How else can I get the facts I need?

Fact Finder: Do you really want to know?

Student: Sure.

Fact Finder: Then let's start at the beginning. What's the first thing to do when making a report?

Student: Copy facts from an encyclopedia or some other book.

Fact Finder: Wrong! The first thing to do is figure out your main question. Every report starts with a question. The facts that you'll collect will help you answer your question.

Student: I didn't know that.

Fact Finder: Now that you do, what question do you want to answer about ice cream?

Student: Gosh, I'm not sure. Let me think about it for a minute. (Student takes the pose of the famous statue called *The Thinker*.)

Fact Finder: Go ahead. Thinking is an important part of writing a good report.

Student: (Snaps fingers.) One question might be "How was ice cream invented?" (Snaps fingers again.) Here's another: "Is it unhealthy to eat ice cream?" (Snaps again). Or "How is ice cream made?"

Fact Finder: Which one interests you the most?

Student: The question about how ice cream is made.

Fact Finder: That's a good question for research.

Student: Great. Now I need some facts, right?

Fact Finder: Right. There are three main ways to gather information. First, you can read.

(Book, Magazine, and Newspaper enter, say their lines, and exit.)

Book: Printed materials like me cover almost everything from aardvarks to zombies. We're very helpful when you're just beginning to learn about a subject.

Student: Wow, a talking book.

Magazine: We're also easy to use.

Newspaper: The only problem is that our words are fixed on paper. We're stuck the way we are. If you don't understand what we say, we can't hear your questions and try again.

Student: (To Fact Finder) Is there anything I can do about that?

Fact Finder: You can use the second way to get facts.

Student: What is it?

Fact Finder: Finding people who know about your subject and asking them questions. If you watch TV news programs, you'll see reporters doing this.

(A reporter with a microphone enters along with an animal trainer.)

Reporter: How do you get the tiger to do a somersault?

Trainer: The secret is in breaking the trick into little steps.

(The reporter jots the answer in a notebook as they leave the stage.)

Fact Finder: You can also interview people by phone or in a letter.

Customer: (Carries phone.) Hello, I'd like to talk to someone about wood stoves?

Student: Hmmm. For my next report, which is about tooth decay, I could call a dentist, and then use the answers to make my report.

Fact Finder: You catch on quickly.

Student: Gosh, that would be a lot more exciting than just copying from a book. But what's the third way of finding facts?

Fact Finder: You use your own eyes or ears.

Student: You mean like a scientist?

Fact Finder: Sure. Many people do this, for example, sports writers.

Sports writer: (Enters with binoculars.) I study the game for myself before I write about it.

Student: So you mean that I might first read a book about how ice cream is made, and then learn more by watching someone actually make it?

Fact Finder: You said it, not me.

Student: But how can I find someone who knows how to make ice cream?

Fact Finder: Think about it.

Student: (Takes the Thinker pose again. Then does another finger snap.) I could call up Irene's Ice Cream shop. Her phone number must be in the directory.

Fact Finder: That makes sense.

Student: The trouble is that it will take more work than just copying from the encyclopedia.

Fact Finder: You're right, but when you use two or three ways of getting facts, your finished report will be more interesting than when you use just one. You'll also learn more.

Student: I think I'll give it a try.

Fact Finder: Good luck.

Student: But how can I thank you?

Fact Finder: Think about it.

(Fact Finder leaves the stage as the student gets into the Thinker pose for the last time.)

Asking Questions

GOAL:
Encouraging curiosity

ACTIVITIES:
1. Use the *Can You See a Question? worksheet* to link observation and questioning skills. Some of the questions generated by this activity could make starting points for actual reports.
2. Turn the results from the *Question Collecting worksheet* into a bulletin board that celebrates the curiosity of students, fellow teachers, and people in the community.
3. As a related activity, set up an ongoing question-collecting bulletin board. Students can select and display the most interesting question of the week or the month.
4. Use the *Two Kinds of Questions worksheet* to help students distinguish between facts and opinions. Reinforce the distinction by explaining that fact-type questions can usually be answered by observation, measurement, or experiment.

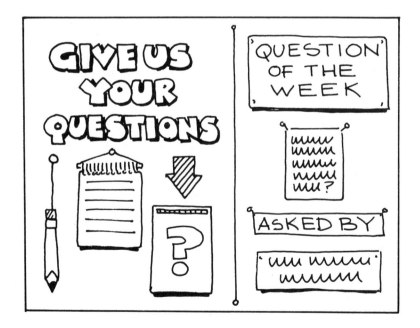

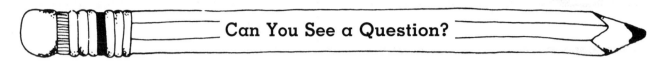

The first step in making a report is finding a question to answer. The better you are at thinking up questions, the better your reports will be.

1. Write as many questions as you can about the things in the picture. A sample has been done for you. If you need more space, use the back of this sheet.

Are all spider webs the same shape?

_____

_____

_____

_____

_____

2. On another sheet of paper, make a list of questions about things that you see in or out of school.

Question Collecting

One way to get better at asking questions is learning about other people's questions. Use the chart below to collect questions from friends, classmates, teachers, neighbors, or anyone else you know. Say to each person something like this:

Will you give me a question that you would like answered?

Name of person	Question

Two Kinds of Questions

When you do research, sometimes you'll ask questions about facts. Other times, you'll ask questions about opinions. It's important to know which is which.

1. A fact is a true statement that can be checked by observing, measuring, or seeing proof. Complete the following questions so that each could be answered by a fact. You don't need to know the answer. A sample has been done for you.

A. Who was the first person to *fly in a jet plane* ?

B. How tall is the _____ ?

C. What colors appear on the flag of _____ ?

D. In what year was the _____ invented?

E. In what city is _____ located?

F. How much does a _____ weigh?

G. How many teeth does a _____ have?

H. How far is _____ from _____ ?

I. Which costs more: a pound of _____ or a pound of _____ ?

J. What is the fastest a _____ has gone?

2. An opinion is what someone believes about something. There is no way to prove an opinion. Complete the following questions so that each asks for an opinion.

A. What is the best _____ ?

B. What do you think would happen if _____ ?

C. What is the worst _____ ?

D. Why did _____ ?

E. Who do you think is the most _____ ?

Exploring the Library

GOAL:
Becoming familiar with the library's contents and organization

ACTIVITIES:
1. Begin with the *What's in the Library? worksheet*, a kind of do-it-yourself guide to the school or local library. Students can write up their findings as a "library report" which might be shared with children in younger grades or with parents.

2. In small or large groups, have students perform the *Dewey Decimal Speeches* to introduce or reinforce the classification system used in most schools and public libraries. You might wish to further distinguish between nonfiction and fiction by displaying examples of each.

3. Make sure students visit each part of the library's nonfiction collection by giving them the *Dewey Decimal Book Hunt worksheet*.

4. To strengthen understanding of book classification, have students create Dewey Decimal posters for the classroom or library. For inspiration, use the *Model Dewey Decimal Poster worksheet*.

5. To help students realize how much information can be obtained from a catalog card, give them the *Reading a Catalog Card worksheet*. After covering the basics, this handout invites students to find their own example by visiting a real card catalog.

Note: In most universities and many city library systems, catalog cards have been replaced by computerized listings. To prepare your students for the electronic library, you might plan a field trip to a library that features a computerized catalog.

6. Use the *Reference Book Speeches* to introduce students to four key resources: the encyclopedia, the almanac, the atlas, and the dictionary.

7. To summarize—and celebrate—what students have learned about the school or town library—have them make a *Library Map bulletin board*. For a model, see the last page in this section.

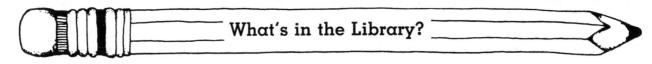 **What's in the Library?**

Many libraries offer more than just books. Take this sheet to your library. See how many things you can find there.

☐ Computer for use by people who visit the library

    types of software: _____

☐ Globe

☐ Magazines: how many different titles _____

☐ Movies (videotapes or films): how many _____

☐ Pictures to loan
    ( ) drawings
    ( ) paintings
    ( ) photographs
    ( ) slides

☐ Recordings to loan (phonograph records or tapes)
    ( ) comedy
    ( ) foreign language lessons
    ( ) music
    ( ) plays
    ( ) other

☐ Reference librarian who can help you find what you need
    Telephone number of reference librarian: _____

☐ Telephone directories of other cities: how many _____

☐ Toys for loan: how many _____

☐ Typewriters: how many _____

☐ Other things: list them on the back of this sheet.

Hello. I'm the Dewey Decimal System. I can help you find books in the library.

I work the way street numbers do. Just as every building in town has a number, each nonfiction book in the library has a number from 000 to 999.

Books about the moon, for example, have a number that starts 523. To find a book's exact number, you look in the card catalog or on a computer screen.

In the Dewey System, all nonfiction books fit into one of ten big number groups.

I'm the *General works* group of books. If I had a nickname it would be "facts."

My numbers go from 000 to 099. On my shelves you'll find books about the library, general encyclopedias like *The World Book* or *Compton's*, almanacs, and trivia books. You'll also find unusual things such as handwritten letters or very old books.

In my part of the library you'll even find books that tell about other books. For example, a book labeled 016 lists books of stories for storytellers.

I'm the *Ideas* group of books. If you want to learn about thinking and feelings, come to me.

My numbers go from 100 to 199. On my shelves you will find books about how people figure out what's true and what's false.

I include books that deal with emotions like love and fear. Also, in my part of the library you can read about good and bad behavior, hypnosis, ESP, and dreams.

There's even a book, whose number is 153, that will help you improve your memory.

I'm the *Religion* group of books. My shelves, which are numbered from 200 to 299, hold books about God and prayer.

This is the part of the library to visit if you're studying Buddhism, Christianity, Hinduism, Islam, Judaism, Shintoism, or other religions.

For example, a book with the title *Bible Stories* has the number 220. Another, called *How the Greek Religions Began*, is numbered 292.

I'm the *Social sciences* group of books, where you can read about how people get along with each other. My numbers go from 300 to 399.

If you want to know about politics, government workers, money, law, crime, education, business, holidays, manners, and folklore, come to me.

On my shelves you'll find a book about equality with the number 301. Another, about fire fighters, is numbered 352. And holidays are covered in a book labeled 372.

I'm the *Languages* group of books. My numbers go from 400 to 499.

Do you want to study German, French, Italian, Spanish, Greek, or some other foreign language? If so, you'll find the right book here. For example, a book on Chinese writing is on my shelves. Its number is 495.

My group includes old languages that aren't even used any more. For example, 493 is the number for hieroglyphics, also known as picture writing.

Of course, if you want to know more about English, come to me. I'm the one to see for dictionaries and books about words.

I'm the *Pure sciences* group of books. My numbers go from 500 to 599.

A pure science is a science that deals with facts about the world, rather than with how to use science to make things.

Among the pure sciences are mathematics, astronomy, physics, chemistry, geology, and biology.

Some of the books you'll find in my part of the library are *Science Experiments*, numbered 507, *Math Puzzles*, numbered 510, *Magnets*, numbered 538, and *Zoos of the World*, numbered 590.

I'm the *Useful sciences* group of books, also known as "technology." My numbers go from 600 to 699.

On my shelves you find books that tell how people use the facts of science in everyday life. Subjects include medicine, engineering, farming, home economics, business, manufacturing, and building.

For example, *How to Be an Inventor* is here; it's numbered 608. A book about *Wind Power* is 621. If you want to read about space travel, look for books marked 629. Books about pets are numbered 636.

I'm the *Arts* group of books. My numbers go from 700 to 799.

The word "art" might make you think of activities like drawing and painting. And it's true, you'll find books on those subjects here. For example, 743 is the number for a book about drawing people.

But the arts also include photography, 770, music, 780, and acting, 792.

On my shelves you'll even find books about games and sports. So, if you're planning to read about chess, look for the number 794. Or if football is your sport, the number is 796.

I'm the *Literature* group of books. My numbers go from 800 to 899.

Here, you'll find plays, poems, letters, jokes, and other kinds of nonfiction writing not covered in the other groups. You will also find writings from all over the world.

Here are a few examples. A book numbered 808 promises it can teach you how to read and write poetry. Another book in the same group presents funny skits you can put on. Then there's an 896 book which is a collection of poems from Africa.

I'm the *History and geography* group of books. My numbers go from 900 to 999.

For example, if you want a travel book, look for one numbered 910. If you're interested in reading about famous people you want something in the biography section, starting with 920.

My other numbers tell about different places. For example, books numbered 940 are about Europe. Asia is covered in the 950s. Africa is 960 and books about North America, including the United States, Canada, and Mexico, are listed in the 970s.

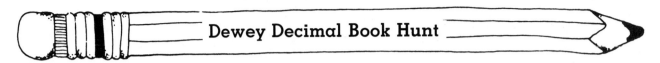
Dewey Decimal Book Hunt

Take this sheet to the library. Find a book for each of the ten Dewey Decimal groups. Write the book's name and Dewey Decimal number in spaces below.

_____

000—099s General works

_____

100—199 Ideas

_____

200—299 Religion

_____

300—399 Social sciences

_____

400—499 Languages

_____

500—599 Pure sciences

_____

600—699 Useful sciences

_____

700—799 Arts

_____

800—899 Literature

_____

900—999 History and geography

_____

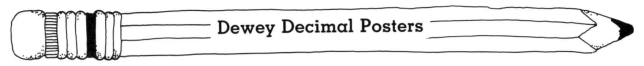

In the General Works group, you will find almanacs, indexes, books about how libraries work, and other materials that help people look for information.

Reading a Catalog Card

Every nonfiction book in a library has a number that helps you find the book. In most libraries, you can find a book's number by looking in the card catalog. For each book there will be three cards: a title card, a subject card, and an author card. The cards are arranged alphabetically, so if you know the book's author, title, or subject, you can easily look up its number.

1. Study the following author card. Then answer the questions below:

```
523.4     Hill, Irwin,      1942
  H             Mars.      Illustrated by
                           Helen Kleeman
               Palo Alto, New Way Books, 1983

               120 pages

               1. Mars     2. Space travel
```

A. What is the title of the book? _____

B. What is the author's last name? _____

C. When was the author born? _____

D. What is the book's Dewey Decimal number? _____

E. In what year was the book published? _____

F. What company published the book? _____

G. Where was the book published? _____

H. How many pages are in the book? _____

2. Go to your school or town library. Look up a card for any nonfiction book. Copy the card onto the back of this sheet.

I'm the *reference section* of the library. I'm where you'll find all sorts of books packed with facts you can use when writing reports.

Most reference books, such as encyclopedias, are made so you can easily find the information you're looking for. They'll help you learn things like the name of the longest river in the world or the first person to fly faster than sound.

One last fact about reference books is that they stay in the library and can't be checked out like other books.

I'm the *general encyclopedia.* I contain articles about thousands of subjects, everything from famous people to strange sea creatures.

The subjects in an encyclopedia are arranged in alphabetical order. Using me is sort of like using a dictionary.

But I'm different from the regular dictionary in one important way. I'm made up of many books, which are called volumes. Each volume covers part of the alphabet. To read about airplanes, you look in the A volume. To learn about zoos, you look in the XYZ volume.

I'm an *almanac.* I contain thousands of short facts about things like awards, disasters, geography, government, history, holidays, population, science, and weather.

Would you like to know how fast the fastest woman can run 100 meters? You'll find it in my pages, along with all sorts of other records. I keep up to date because each year a new almanac is published.

I'm an *atlas.* I'm good at helping people find facts about the world. I give information about things like cities, countries, highways, rivers, mountains, oceans, lakes, and climate.

Many of my pages are filled with maps. Some of the maps show the way things are today. Others show how things used to be. By studying changes on the maps, you can often learn a great deal about how the world is changing.

I'm a *general dictionary.* I tell how words are spelled and how they're pronounced. But I can do more than that, such as showing how different words are related. For example, did you know that "portable" and "important" come from the same root?

In addition to general dictionaries, there are dictionaries for special subjects.

Bulletin Board

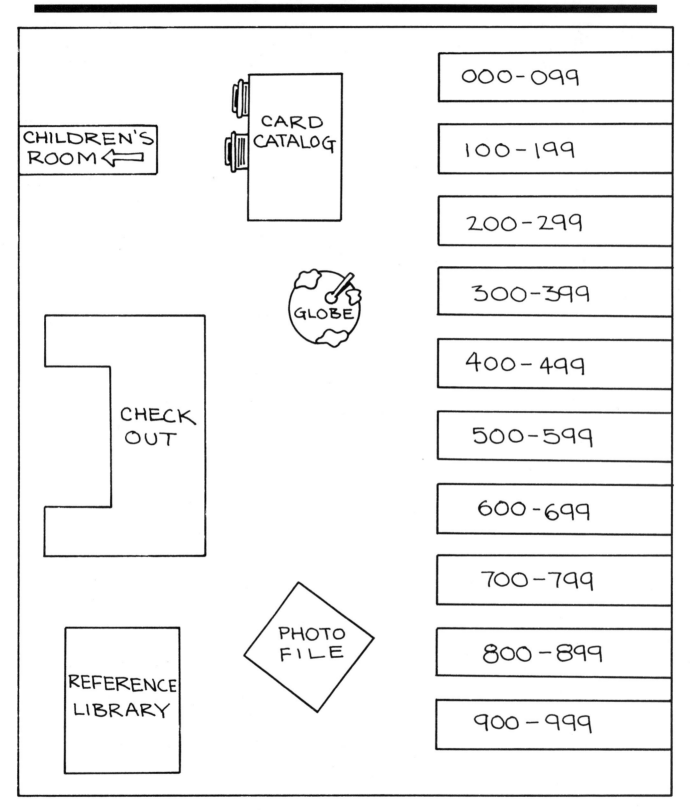

CHILDREN'S ROOM ←

CARD CATALOG

GLOBE

CHECK OUT

PHOTO FILE

REFERENCE LIBRARY

000-099
100-199
200-299
300-399
400-499
500-599
600-699
700-799
800-899
900-999

Have students reinforce their study of the library by helping you produce a map of the school or the town's library.

Using Books

GOAL:
Learning to get the most out of nonfiction books

TEACHING TIPS:
1. Use the following worksheets to familiarize students with the basic elements of a nonfiction book: *Reading a Contents Page*, *Reading an Index*, *Reading a Bibliography*, and *Reading a Fact Table*.
2. Give students note-taking practice by using the *Taking Notes worksheet*. After students list eight or ten facts, have them tear the sheet along the dotted line, giving you the article part and keeping the notes for themselves. A few days later, have the students use their notes to recreate the material. They can then compare their version with the original. This activity, obviously, should be repeated frequently using nonfiction material from textbooks, newspapers, magazines, encyclopedias, and other sources.

  **Reading a Contents Page**

A book's contents page can tell you a lot about the book. See for yourself. Answer the following questions about the contents page below. It's from a book called *Fun with Magic*.

Contents

Introduction	1
Chapter 1. Practicing Magic	3
Chapter 2. Ten Easy Card Tricks	7
Chapter 3. Mind-reading with Cats and Dogs	23
Chapter 4. Magic For Two Magicians	29
Chapter 5. Musical Magic	39
Chapter 6. Giggle-making Magic	49
Chapter 7. Fooling with Food Tricks	59
Bibliography: Other Books on Easy Magic	67
Index	71

1. How many chapters are in the book? _____

2. Which chapter tells about card tricks? _____

3. Which chapter tells about making people laugh? _____

4. Which chapter teaches about mind reading? _____

5. Which chapter talks about practice? _____

6. On which page does the bibliography begin? _____

7. Which chapter has to do with music? _____

8. Which is the longest chapter in the book? _____

An index comes at the back of a book and helps you find *the exact page* you need. It lists every topic in alphabetical order, and gives the page or pages where you'll find that topic. Each item in the index is called an *entry*. Here's an example:

Milk, 3, 9-12

This entry means you can read about milk on pages 3, 9, 10, 11, and 12.

1. Answer the following questions about the sample index on the right.

A. On which page will you find facts about *Lights*?

_____

B. On which pages can you read about *Wheels*?

_____

C. How many pages deal with *Tricycles*?

_____

D. If there were an entry for *Speed* in this index, which entry would it follow?

_____

E. Which topic comes on a page that's closer to the front of the book— *Motor bikes* or *Seats*?

_____

F. There is no entry for flat tires, but which entries might deal with that subject?

_____

Index from *The Bike Book*

Accidents, 22-26
Bicycle-built-for-two, 15
Chain, 9, 13
Champion riders, 37-38
Equipment, 2, 7, 12, 44, 47
Fixing, 11-20
Handlebars, 6
Helmet, 2, 24
History, 5-16
Lights, 47
Motor bikes, 25
Movies, 67-76
Night riding, 45-48
Other countries, 64-66
Pedals, 8
Racing, 31-38, 64-66
Reflector repairing, 11-20
Safety, 21-30
Seats, 7
Spokes, 5
Tires, 5, 6
Tricks, 20, 22
Tricycles, 8, 10
Trips, 49-66
Wheels, 4-6

2. Find a book that has an index. Write its name here:

_____

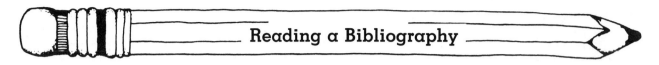

A bibliography is a list of books and other materials used by a writer. The bibliography shows where the writer got his or her facts. It helps readers who want to learn more about the subject.

1. Answer the following questions, which are about the sample bibliography.

A. In what city was Ellen Strong's book published? _____

B. Who wrote *How to Sell an Invention*? _____

C. Which company published *Gadgets*? _____

D. What is the year of the oldest item on the list? _____

E. Which items are *not* books? _____

Bibliography (from a book about inventions)

1. Arthur, Linda, *Inventors Behind the Movies Move*, Bell Books, New Orleans, 1981.

2. Brown, Lawrence, *How to Sell an Invention*, Gallaxy Books, Seattle, 1981.

3. Mayer, Vicki, letter to the author, dated March 21, 1983.

4. Mitchell, Thomas, *Gadgets*, Summer Press, Orlando, 1979.

5. Nathan, Richard, *The Story of an Invention: a Channel 24 news special*, NBR Cable-TV Movie, first presented on July 19, 1985.

6. Strong, Ellen, *How to Be an Inventor*, New Way Books, Chicago, 1984.

7. Williamson, Maynard, *The Ten Greatest Inventions of All Time*, Dakota Books, New York, 1986.

8. Winter, Karl, *How Did Edison Invent so Much?*, Star Books, Toronto, 1976.

2. Find a book with a bibliography. Write its name here:

_____

A fact table presents facts in rows (across) and columns (down). Tables are useful because they pack a lot of information into a small space. You'll find them in many places including almanacs, encyclopedias, newspapers, and magazines.

1. Answer the following questions about the table below:

A. What is the table's title? _____

B. What is the continent of the third longest river? _____

C. Does this table tell how to pronounce the rivers' names? _____

D. On which continent is the world's longest river? _____

E. Which continent has most of the longest rivers? _____

F. In miles, how much longer is the Nile than the Amazon? _____

G. If someone discovered a new river that was 4,690 kilometers long, which river would it follow on the table? _____

World's 10 Longest Rivers			
Name	Continent	Length Miles	Kilometers
Nile	Africa	4,145	6,671
Amazon	South America	4,000	6,437
Yangtze	Asia	3,915	6,300
Huang Ho	Asia	2,903	4,672
Congo	Africa	2,900	4,667
Amur	Asia	2,744	4,416
Lena	Asia	2,734	4,400
Irtysh	Asia	2,640	4,248
Mackenzie	North America	2,635	4,241
Mekong	Asia	2,600	4,184

2. Find a table in a magazine, newspaper, or book. On the back of this sheet, tell the name of the table and give one row of facts.

When you take notes, write only the most important facts. Later, you can rewrite these facts in your own words. In the lines below, take notes on the following article.

Philo T. Farnsworth

The thirteen-year-old boy riding the horse-drawn hay mower was named Philo Farnsworth. As he went up and down the rows of his family's Idaho farm, Philo was thinking about an invention that would change the world.

While you may never have heard of Philo Farnsworth, you certainly know about his invention. That day back in 1919, Philo was dreaming about inventing television.

Television! The word was still so new back then that most people had never even heard of it. Science fiction writers of the time were still writing about the coming age of radio. Television seemed almost like magic.

Yet, within eight years, Philo would build a machine that would send moving pictures from one place to another.

Learning from People

GOAL:
Using interviewing, polling, and letter writing to gather information

ACTIVITIES:
1. To help students discover that people can be a valuable resource, let them work with the *Finding Experts worksheet*.

2. To introduce interviewing, use the *Model Interview worksheet* as a script which students can read aloud with partners. Point out the importance of follow-up questions such as "How do you do that?"

3. Have the class help you stage a live interview in the room, following the steps on the *Interview Planner worksheet*. For an interviewee, you might select a colleague who has an interesting hobby or who has traveled widely. During the interview, model the art of asking follow-up questions.

4. Have students sharpen their own interview skills by interviewing classmates on topics like hobbies or skills. To extend the activity outside the classroom, students can interview family members, neighbors, and people in the community.

5. For an initial polling activity, conduct a classroom poll using the *Pet Poll worksheet*. Later, students can use the same worksheet to practice polling with neighbors. Of course, students should eventually take their own polls on such topics as favorite TV shows, favorite foods, and favorite holidays.

6. To help prevent telephone-o-phobia, have students do mock telephone interviews in the classroom.

7. Conducting research by mail is a powerful fact-finding technique; it also provides practice in writing business letters. Encourage your young researchers to seek information from companies producing foods, toys, and other familiar items. See the *Research Letter worksheet* for a model. While some addresses appear on labels or packages, you might also ask students to locate library reference books that give business addresses.

 **Finding Experts**

Whatever subject you're researching, you can almost always find someone who can give you the facts you need. The trick is being willing to search for the right person.

1. Try to find the name of a person who could give you information on each of the subjects below. Hint: Ask your friends or relatives for names.

How to fix a car

What it's like to pilot an airplane

What it's like to be a high school student

How to fix a drippy faucet

How to dive off a high diving board

How to build a model airplane

What it's like to be on a TV show

What it's like to travel in a foreign country

2. On the back, list a few subjects you're interested in. Then try to find a person who knows about each subject.

Model Interview

1. Here's part of an interview with a banker. To learn how an interview works, read the page aloud with a partner. One of you can ask the questions and the other read the answers.

Stopping Bank Robberies
an interview by Sandy Watson

Have you ever wondered what banks do to avoid robberies? I did. To find the answers I interviewed the security officer at First City Bank.

Question: Are bank robberies much of a problem?

Answer: At some banks, yes, but we haven't had one for five years, thank goodness.

Question: Does that mean you don't worry about robberies?

Answer: Not at all. My job is to worry and to think of ways to stop robberies from happening.

Question: How do you do that?

Answer: I can't tell you everything, but one trick is to stare at suspicious-looking people. Robbers hate to be looked at, so staring can scare them away.

Question: Do you train your tellers to use guns?

Answer: No.

Question: Why not?

Answer: We don't want shooting in the bank because customers or our workers could be hurt.

2. On the back of this sheet, list three or four other questions that you would ask the banker if you were doing the interview.

CAROL COOK
SECURITY OFFICER

Interview Planner

Here are the steps to follow when you want to interview someone.

1. Name the subject you're researching: _____

2. Name the person you will interview: _____

3. Set the date, time, and place of the interview:

_____

4. Decide how you will record what the person says:
   ☐ using paper and pencil
   ☐ using a tape recorder

5. List between five and ten important questions you want to ask the person. Of course, you may think up other questions during the interview.

_____

_____

_____

_____

_____

_____

6. During the interview, if something isn't clear, ask a follow-up question such as "Why did you do that?" or "How did that happen?"

7. When the interview is over, thank the person for taking the time to answer your questions.

Pet Poll

When you take a poll, you ask many people one or a few questions. You mark their answers on a sheet like the one below. For each answer, draw a tally mark (**|**) in the right box. After four marks, draw a line through the tallies to show five (JHt).

Before asking your questions, explain what you're doing:
    I'm taking a poll for a school project. I hope you'll
    have a few seconds to answer a question or two. Thanks.

1. Do you have a pet?	Boys	Girls
Yes		
No		
If the answer is "Yes," ask question 2.		
2. What kind of pet is it?	Boys	Girls
Dog		
Cat		
Bird		
Mouse		
Snake		
Other (name it)		

 **Research Letter**

One way to get facts is to send a research letter to someone who knows about your subject.

1. Study the model research letter below.

1111 Greenwood Avenue
Palo Alto, CA 94301
February 1, 1986

Public Relations Office
Sunny Soap Company
Sudsville, North Dakota 77009

Dear Sunny Soap Company:

I am working on a report about hand soap. I have not been able to learn the answer to the following question:

How does the soap's name get printed on each bar?

I hope you will be able to answer my question. Thanks for your help.

Sincerely,

Bobby Ryan

Bobby Ryan

---

2. Think up a question that a company might be able to answer. On the back of this paper, write a letter to the company and ask your question. Be sure that your letter includes the eight parts shown in the model letter. When your letter reads the way you want it to, make a clean copy.

Observing

GOAL:
Teaching students to use their own senses to gather information

ACTIVITIES:
1. To help students understand that observation requires a focus, use the *Knowing What to Look For worksheet.*
2. For practice in careful observation, give students the *Alike and Different worksheet.* Extend the activity by using objects such as two vases or two pictures of similar scenes.
3. Use the *Drawing What You See worksheet* to show students that sketching can increase observation power. Repeat this important activity using drawings found in newspapers, magazines, and books.
4. To extend the previous activities, have each student keep a verbal and visual log of what occurs outside a given window at a given time. The activity might go on for a month or more.
5. For practice in recording an event, have students write everything they see and hear during a brief period—say a minute—of watching a TV show, a TV commercial, or a movie.
6. Have students use the *High and Low Temperature Graph worksheet* to collect and organize data. Discuss how the placement of the thermometer—in full sun versus in the shade—will affect the readings. Suggest ways of sharing the data, for example, on a bulletin board.
7. Use the *Attendance Graph worksheet* for practice in social studies research. After a few weeks, ask students to write up their findings. For example, they might point out a pattern of lower attendance on certain days of the week. (An interesting variation would be to make separate charts for boys and girls.) You might have students use the data in reports to parents.

Oct. 2 9:30 a.m. It's a calm day.

Oct. 9 9:30 a.m. Someone left trash on the ground

Oct. 16 9:30 a.m. It's windy. Someone has parked in the no parking zone.

In the spaces below, write down the different kinds of things you see in the picture:

Animals _____

Plants _____

Metal things _____

Wood things _____

Signs _____

Noisy things _____

Movable things _____

Things to eat _____

Alike and Different

Study the two leaves on this page. Then tell all the ways they are alike and all the ways they are different.

The two leaves are *alike* in these ways:

_____

_____

_____

_____

The two leaves are *different* in these ways:

_____

_____

_____

_____

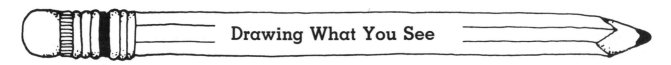

Making a simple sketch of what you see can help you see more. You don't have to be a good artist to do it. See for yourself.

1. Make your own sketch of each of the following drawings.

2. On the back of this sheet, draw something that is in your classroom or in your home.

High and Low Temperature Graph

Use this chart to keep track of the high and the low temperature during the school day. Mark the high temperature with a red dot and the low temperature with a blue dot. Under each day at the bottom of the chart, mark the date, for example, May 3.

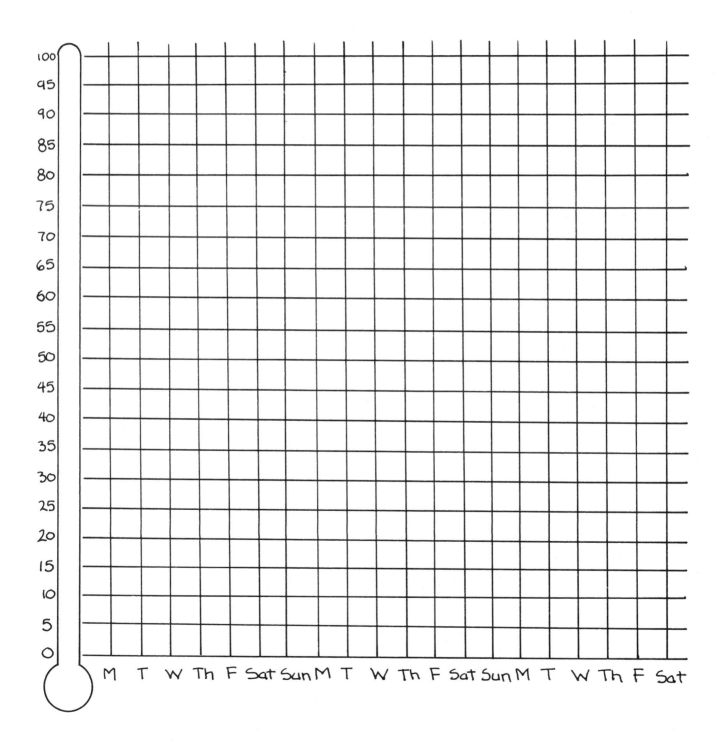

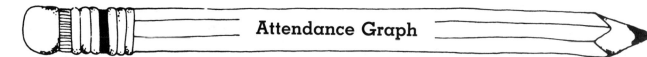

Attendance Graph

Use this graph to keep track of how many students come to class each day.

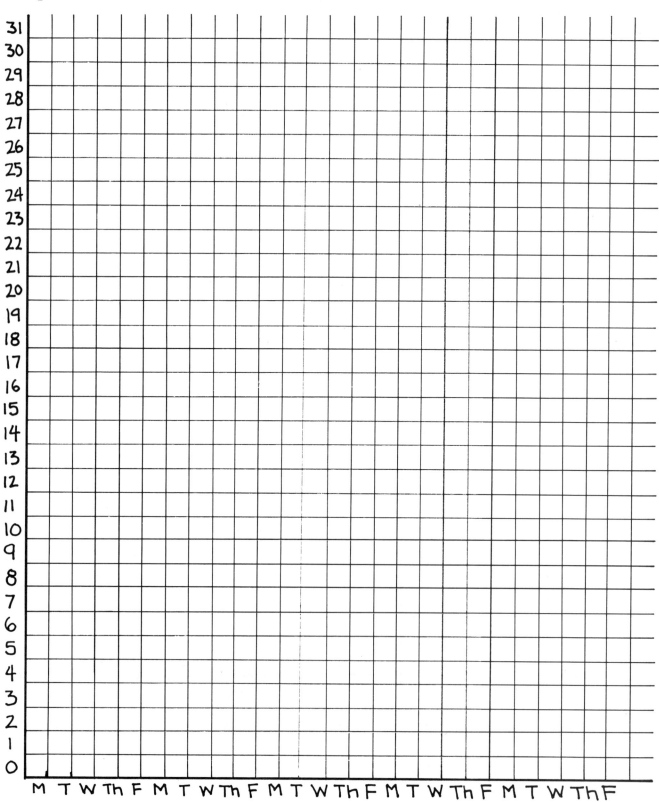

Giving Reports

GOAL:
Exploring ways to share information

ACTIVITIES:
1. Arrange for students to see experienced speakers give lecture-style reports. One source of presenters would be students from a high school speech class or debate club.
2. When it's time for students to prepare reports, give them the step-by-step *Report Checklist worksheet*.
3. To introduce students to footnoted reports, have them study the *Model Report worksheet*. This example includes facts gathered from a variety of sources including phone calls and original documents. Point out to students how much information can be packed onto a single page. For more involvement, you might ask questions about the model. For example:

    A. Which footnotes refer to sources that had to be read?
    B. How many facts came from the newspaper?
    C. Which footnotes refer to telephone conversations?

4. Because students are often nervous the first time they present oral reports, arrange for them to give "second time" presentations to other classes. This activity will be more feasible if the reports are short, lasting perhaps two or three minutes.
5. For a less traditional approach to reporting facts, have students use the *Bulletin Board Checklist worksheet*. This format offers a way for students to share their research findings with other students and teachers throughout the school.

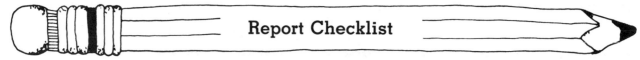

Here are ten steps to follow when preparing a research report. Check each box when you've completed the step.

☐ **1.** What is the main question your report will answer? _____

_____

☐ **2.** Give the date when the report is due: _____

☐ **3.** Check the form your finished report will take:
    ( ) Written
    ( ) Plain speech
    ( ) Speech that includes showing pictures or objects

☐ **4.** List the sources you will use in doing your research. Include people you will talk to and things you plan to observe for yourself. (If you need more space, use the back.)

_____

_____

☐ **5.** After doing your research, list the important facts you plan to present. If you need more space, use the back.

_____

_____

_____

☐ **6.** If you're going to include pictures or things, list them:

_____

_____

☐ **7.** Write your report. Be sure to give it an interesting title.

☐ **8.** If you're going to give an oral report, rehearse it two ways:
    ( ) by yourself, perhaps using a tape recorder
    ( ) in front of a friend or relative

☐ **9.** Hand in your report or give your speech.

☐ **10.** On the back of this paper, write a few sentences that tell what was good about your report and what could have been better.

The Big News of November 14, 1975
by Andrew Loomis

Around sunrise on November 14, 1975, a two-alarm fire burned down an empty factory on River Road. Later that day, Jefferson High School's football team won its seventh game in a row.[1]

I knew nothing of this. In fact, I wasn't even around until 8:29 P.M. when I arrived at Memorial Hospital.[2] Dr. Ellen Daniels was there to help me arrive. She doesn't remember much about my birth, saying only, "It must not have been very unusual."[3]

My mother and father remember the day, but that's not too surprising. I was their first child. My father says he especially recalls the day because "Your birth meant that I left work early."[4]

My mother remembers that it was a very cold day. In fact, the temperature set a record—8 degrees—that has never been broken.[5]

The only other big news on November 14, 1975, was that our school, Washington School, opened its doors for the first time.[6]

Footnotes

1. *Times-Tribune*, November 14, 1975, page 1.
2. Birth certificate for Andrew Loomis.
3. Dr. Ellen Daniels, letter to the author dated February 2, 1985.
4. Barry Loomis (my father) in a conversation on January 7, 1985.
5. Henry Ringer (weather forecaster) in a phone call with the author, January 8, 1985.
6. Plaque that hangs by the front door of the Washington School.

Bulletin Board Checklist

One way to share what you learn from research is to make a bulletin board. Here are seven steps to follow.

☐ **1.** Bulletin boards work best when they have only one main idea. What idea do you want your board to present? Write it here:

_____

☐ **2.** What do you want people to do when they see your board?
( ) just look at it
( ) try to answer a question
( ) something else

☐ **3.** Plan the look of your board. Will it have:
( ) one big picture?
( ) several smaller pictures?

☐ **4.** Sketch how you want the bulletin board to look. This will include where the picture or pictures will go and where the words will go. Put your sketch on the back.

☐ **5.** Get the picture or pictures you'll need. Will you:
( ) draw them from scratch?
( ) copy them from a newspaper, book, or magazine?
( ) take them with a camera?

☐ **6.** Write the words. Do you want to include:
( ) a title or headline?
( ) words that explain each picture?
( ) a piece of writing that gives more information?

☐ **7.** Put the board up.

Library Scavenger Hunts

GOAL:
Becoming adept at using key reference books

ACTIVITIES:
1. Because library scavenger hunts rely heavily on reference books, prepare students with the *Reference Book Hunt worksheet.*
2. For practice in finding quotations, use the *Quotation Hunt worksheet.*
3. For practice in tracking down visual information, use the *What Does It Look Like? worksheet.*
4. For practice in using an atlas, use the *Mystery Maps worksheet.*
5. For a mixed-bag fact-finding experience, use the *Finding All Kinds of Facts worksheet.*
6. Don't stop now. Have students create their own scavenger-hunt worksheets to challenge their classmates, their parents, and — even — their teachers.

A reference book is a book you turn to when you want facts in a hurry. Here's a chance for you to get to know about some important reference books. Visit a library, find the reference section, and fill out this sheet.

1. Name two quotation books.

_____

2. Name a book that lists addresses of businesses like General Motors or Apple Computers.

_____

3. Name an atlas.

_____

4. Name two general encyclopedias.

_____

5. Name a biographical dictionary. This is a dictionary that lists facts about all kinds of famous people.

_____

6. Name an almanac that contains facts about all kinds of subjects including cities, countries, animals, and people.

_____

7. Name a book that gives facts about the first time things happened, for example, the first time someone used a parachute.

_____

8. Name a book that's filled with facts about sports.

_____

9. Name a book that contains facts about writers.

_____

10. On the back of this sheet, name any other special fact book.

Quotation Hunt

A quotation is a sentence or a few sentences usually taken from a book or a speech. Often a quotation can add interest to a report. Most quotation books are organized in a way that lets you look up quotations either by subject or by the person who is being quoted.

Happiness is a warm puppy.

BOOK OF QUOTES

1. Use quotation books to find a quotation from the following people:

A. Benjamin Franklin _____

_____

B. Anne Frank _____

_____

C. Martin Luther King _____

_____

D. Helen Keller _____

_____

2. Find a quotation about the following subjects. Tell who said the words.

Food _____

_____

_____

Learning _____

_____

_____

Television _____

_____

_____

Any other subject of your choice _____

_____

What Does It Look Like?

In some reports, you'll need to show readers what your subject looks like. You can often do this by copying a picture or drawing one from scratch.

1. Use an encyclopedia, a dictionary, or other book to find the following things. Then draw them in the boxes.

an amoeba

the Leaning Tower of Pisa

a dormer window

an outline map of India

2. On the back of this sheet, draw a picture of the front of your school.

Mystery Maps

Study the clues in each of the following maps. Then, find the missing facts using an atlas or an encyclopedia.

1. Name this city: _____
2. Name this river: _____

_____

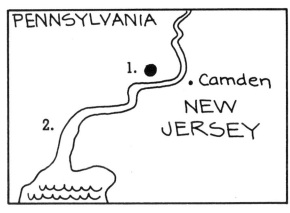

3. Name this province: _____
4. Name this city: _____
5. Name this lake: _____

_____

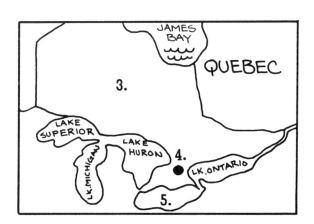

6. Name this country: _____
7. Name this city: _____
8. Name this sea: _____

_____

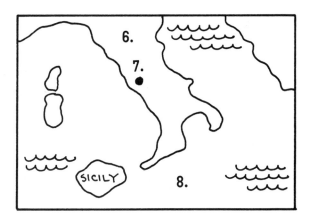

 **Finding All Kinds of Facts**

Use books, people, or your own senses to complete this page. When you're asked to give the source, tell how you found the fact or facts.

1. Name two books that tell how to spell the capital of Canada.

_____

_____

2. What is the phone number of city hall in your town?

_____ Source: _____

3. Who wrote the book *The Cat in the Hat*?

_____ Source: _____

4. In what country is Timbuktu located?

_____ Source: _____

5. What is the zip code of the United Nations in New York City?

_____ Source: _____

6. Give the title of a painting by Grant Wood.

_____ Source: _____

7. What is the real name of Lewis Carroll?

_____ Source: _____

8. Who was Julius Caesar?

_____ Source: _____

9. Give the address of the company that makes the hand soap or bath soap used in your home.

_____ Source: _____

10. What does the French phrase *au revoir* mean?

_____ Source: _____

Double-checking the Facts

GOAL:
Learning to be accurate

ACTIVITIES:
1. Introduce this important research and editing activity with an "Is It True?" bulletin board. Once a week or so, post a statement, which students will double-check and comment on by adding cards either agreeing with the statement or correcting the statement. Whether the fact is correct or not, each note must have a source.
2. Give students worksheets filled with statements to double-check. To ensure that students consult many sources, include topics like:

In Morse Code, the signal for the letter "M" is three dots.
Mark Spitz won nine gold medals at the 1968 Olympics.
Venus is the planet closest to the sun.
The flag of Costa Rica has five stripes.
Joy Hill was the first woman to serve in the United States Senate.

3. Occasionally give students manuscripts to check. For starters, use the *What's the Real Story? worksheet.*
4. For continuing practice, have students create their own "You check the facts" materials for classmates to work on.

The following article contains many errors. Check each statement you're not sure of by reading about the Eiffel Tower in an encyclopedia or other source. When you find something wrong, cross it out and write in the correct information. A sample has been done for you. If you're not sure about a fact, put a question mark next to it.

The Eiffel Tower

The Eiffel Tower is one of the most famous landmarks in the world. Located in ~~London,~~ *Paris* it's what most people think of when they hear the word "England."

Alexander Eugene Eiffel, born in 1830, was a teacher who planned and built this amazing structure. The work began in 1877 and was finished in time for the World's Fair of 1879. Many people at the time said that the huge, wooden tower was a waste of money. Within a year, though, sightseers spent enough money to pay for the building's one million dollar price tag.

The Tower, which stands 1,042 feet high, is one of the tallest buildings in Europe. Escalators take tourists to observation decks at four levels. From up there, people have a dramatic view of London and the Danube River.

Trivia

GOAL:
Researching for fun and learning

ACTIVITIES:
1. Have students write trivia items for an ongoing "Did You Know?" feature appearing in the school paper or home-school newsletter. Topics might range from sports and literature to science, pop culture, geography, current events, and more.
2. Read aloud similar material to brighten the morning announcements.
3. Set up a continuing "Trivia" bulletin board, perhaps featuring facts from traditional reports.
4. Have each student write and illustrate a page for a class trivia book. Place a copy of the book in the school library. You might even print enough copies to send home for parents to enjoy.
5. Have students write new question cards for a game like Trivial Pursuits. Of course, some students may prefer to design entirely new games.
6. For more drama, use such material for an in-school quiz show based on popular TV programs such as "Jeopardy" or "The College Bowl." You can play the games in the classroom or at an assembly. You might even try a special "try to stump the teachers" version.

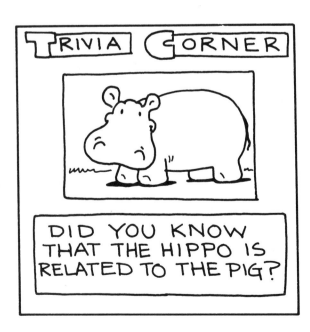

Encyclopedia Reports

GOAL:
Finding creative ways to use encyclopedias and similar references

ACTIVITIES:
1. In general, avoid asking students to make a report based on a single encyclopedia article. That kind of project frequently leads to mindless copying. To promote higher level thinking, have students *compare* two short articles on the same subject. (The shorter the articles the better—especially at first.) The task requires three steps, which should be demonstrated by the teacher. Here's an example using two articles about the saxophone:

Step 1. List the main facts in each article.

Article 1

invented 1877
invented by Antoine Saxe
wind instrument
four kinds
used in French army

Article 2

invented 1877
invented by Antoine Saxe
important in jazz
Charlie Parker

Step 2. Put the facts into a Venn diagram, a strategy that simplifies the task of determining similarities and differences.

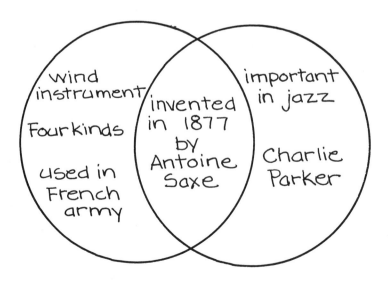

Step 3. Write a short report that tells which facts are found in both articles and which only in one or the other.

2. If your school has old and new editions of the same encyclopedia, have them compare old and new articles on the same subject. Be sure to pick a subject in a rapidly changing field, for example, airplanes, medicine, computers, or fashion.

3. Have students compare two different but related subjects not covered in the same article. Possibilities include:

> two sports such as baseball and football
> two people in the same field, for example, two poets
> two cities such as Montreal and New York
> two kinds of fruit such as apples and oranges

Begin by figuring out the categories by which the items can be compared. One way to do this is to read both articles and then make a chart. For example, in comparing two animals such as the skunk and the porcupine, categories might include:

	skunk	porcupine
appearance		
habitat		
food		
enemies		
defenses		
length of life		

4. Have students write encyclopedia-like articles but with strictly original material. The secret is choosing a subject *not* found in the encyclopedia, for example, a parent, a teacher, a friend, or even a pet. The finished piece should resemble a real encyclopedia in look and tone. It might even end with study questions.

Destination: Earth!

GOAL:
Learning to carry out a major research project

ACTIVITIES:
For this project students pretend to be visitors from another planet. They gather information about Earth from books, interviews, and observation. They then publish their findings about life on earth in individual books or by contributing to a big class book.

1. Use the *A Visit to the Planet Earth worksheet* to introduce the overall project.

2. Use the following three worksheets—*Poll About Space Visitors*, *Earth Places*, and *Earth People* as model pages for the visit-to-Earth book. Students can then use similar formats for covering a wide variety of other topics. You might require that each student-made worksheet focus on a single question. Some questions will be answered through book research. Others will require interviewing and observing. Possibilities include:

Arts: What are some of the best paintings by Earthlings?
Clothing: How has Earth clothing changed over the years? How does Earth clothing vary from one part of the planet to another?
Entertainment: How do Earthlings amuse themselves?
Food: What do Earthlings eat? (This could take the form of a world map showing different foods in different areas.)
Games and Sports: What are the favorite Earth sports? (a poll) When were various Earth sports invented?
Geography: What are the special places on Earth?
Health and Medicine: What do Earthlings do to stay healthy? (a poll or interviews with doctors)
Heroes and Celebrities: Who are the greatest Earthlings in history?
Household Gadgets: How did _____ get invented?
Laws: How are Earth laws made? What are the most important Earth laws? (a poll)
Religion: How are different Earth religions alike and different?
Schooling: What is a typical school day on Earth?
Shopping: What do Earthlings do with their money?
Work: What are the most dangerous jobs? What are the most important jobs? (a poll)

A Visit to the Planet Earth

Some day people from another planet may come to Earth. If that happens, they probably will want to learn how we live. Pretend that you are one of those space people. Your job will be to collect all kinds of facts about life on Earth. When you're done, you will put all the facts into a book.

1. If you came from another planet, you'd have a different name. What

might it be? _____

2. Space visitors might come with many questions about life on earth. Write at least five questions you think they might ask. A sample has been done for you.

Why do Earth people fight each other?

_____

_____

_____

_____

_____

_____

_____

_____

3. On the back of this paper, draw a picture for the cover of your book about the visit to Earth.

 **Poll About Space Visitors**

As a space visitor, you might like to know how Earth people (Earthlings) feel about your visit. To find out, take a poll. Ask at least 10 Earthlings the following questions.

1. Do you think that people from another planet will ever come to Earth?

never _____

maybe someday _____

don't know _____

2. If space visitors did come to Earth, why do you think they would come here? (You can choose more than one item.)

to be friends _____

to make war _____

to trade _____

to learn from
Earthlings _____

to teach
Earthlings _____

no opinion _____

other reasons _____

_____

_____

Earth Places

1. Visit an Earth library and find these important facts about Earth. You might have to use several books such as an almanac, an atlas, and an encyclopedia. Give the name of the book and the page number where you find each fact.

A. How many oceans are there on Earth?

_____ Source _____

B. Where is the hottest place on Earth and how hot does it get?

_____ Source _____

C. What is the coldest place on Earth and how cold does it get?

_____ Source _____

D. What is the tallest mountain on Earth and where is it?

_____ Source _____

E. What place on Earth gets the most rainfall and how much is it?

_____ Source _____

F. What Earth city contains the most people? How many live there?

_____ Source _____

2. Name the town where your spaceship landed: _____

G. When was the town founded?

_____ Source _____

H. How many people live in the town?

_____ Source _____

I. What is the town's highest and lowest recorded temperatures?

_____ Source _____

J. How far is the town above sea level?

_____ Source _____

Answer the following basic questions about Earth people. You may need to use several books such as *The Guinness Book of World Records* and a general almanac such as *Information Please*. In the Source blank, give the book and page number where you found the fact.

1. How many people live on Earth?

_____ Source _____

2. How many languages do Earthlings speak?

_____ Source _____

3. What's the greatest age an Earth person has reached?

_____ Source _____

4. How tall is the tallest Earth person?

_____ Source _____

5. What's the fastest an Earthling has run (in miles per hour)?

_____ Source _____

6. In the boxes below, draw a picture of the human eye and the human ear. Under each picture, tell some of the ways each part is used.

Classroom Reference Shelf

While nothing can replace the library, most researchers like to have a few key references close at hand. Books like those listed here should excite students about research.

Almanacs
Information Please Almanac (Macmillan).
World Almanac and Book of Facts (Newspaper Enterprise Association).

Atlas
National Geographic Atlas of the World (National Geographic Society).

Dictionaries
Webster's Biographical Dictionary (Merriam Webster).
What's What: A visual glossary of everything from paper clips to dinosaurs by Reginald Brangonier and David Fisher (Ballantine).

Encyclopedia
World Book Encyclopedia (World Book, Inc.).

Quotation book
Bartlett's Familiar Quotations by John Bartlett (Little, Brown).

Telephone books
Try to collect some from distant cities. The local *Yellow Pages* are especially valuable for tapping live sources.

Trivia books
Book of Firsts by Patrick Robertson (Clarkson N. Potter).
Book of Lists by David Wallechinsky, et al. (Bantam).
Dictionary of Misinformation by Tom Burnham (Ballantine).
Famous First Facts by Joseph Kane (H.W. Wilson).
Guinness Book of World Records by Norris McWhirter (Bantam). For younger students, there's a series of simplified versions such as *The Guinness Book of Startling Acts and Facts* (Sterling Books).
Incredible Structures by James Myers (Hart Publishing).
People's Almanac by David Wallechinsky et al. (Doubleday).

Answer Key

Page 22: Reading a Catalog Card
- A. *Mars*
- B. Hill
- C. 1942
- D. 523.4 (The letter H stands for the H author's last name.)
- E. 1983
- F. New Way Books
- G. Palo Alto
- H. 120 pages

Page 26: Reading a Contents Page
1. 7 chapters
2. Chapter 2
3. Chapter 6
4. Chapter 3
5. Chapter 1
6. page 67
7. Chapter 5
8. Chapter 2

Page 27: Reading an Index
1. 47
- B. 4, 5, 6
- C. two pages
- D. Seats
- E. Seats
- F. Fixing/Tires

Page 28: Reading a Bibliography
- A. Chicago
- B. Lawrence Brown
- C. Summer Press
- D. 1976
- E. Items 3 and 5

Page 29: Reading a Fact Table
- A. World's 10 Longest Rivers
- B. Asia
- C. No
- D. Africa
- E. Asia
- F. 145 miles
- G. Yangtze

Page 51: Mystery Maps
1. Philadelphia
2. Delaware
3. Ontario
4. Toronto
5. Erie
6. Italy
7. Rome
8. Mediterranean

Page 52: Finding All Kinds of Facts
3. Dr. Seuss
4. Mali
5. 10017
6. American Gothic
7. Charles Lutwidge Dodgson
8. a Roman emperor
10. goodbye

Page 54: What's the Real Story?
- line 3 *England* should be *France*
- line 4 *Eugene* should be *Gustave*
- line 4 *1830* should be *1832*
- line 4 *a teacher* should be *an engineer*
- line 5 *1877* should be *1887*
- line 6 *1879* should be *1889*
- line 7 *wooden* should be *steel*
- line 10 *1042* should be *1052*
- line 11 *escalators* should be *elevators*
- line 11 *four* should be *three*
- line 12 *London* should be *Paris*; *Danube* should be *Seine*

Page 61: Earth Places
1. four oceans
- B. Lybia, about 136 degrees F
- C. Antarctica, about -127. degrees F
- D. Mt. Everest, Tibet-Nepal
- E. India, 1042 inches in a year
- F. Shanghai, around 11 million people

Page 62: Earth People
1. 4,766,000,000.
2. around 3000
3. 114 years
4. 9 feet, 3 inches
5. 27 m.p.h.